OTHER PEOPLE'S
CLERIHEWS

Other People's

CLERIHEWS

Chosen by

GAVIN EWART

With Illustrations by

NICOLA JENNINGS

Oxford   New York

OXFORD UNIVERSITY PRESS

1983

Oxford University Press, Walton Street, Oxford OX2 6DP

London   Glasgow   New York   Toronto
Delhi   Bombay   Calcutta   Madras   Karachi
Kuala Lumpur   Singapore   Hong Kong   Tokyo
Nairobi   Dar es Salaam   Cape Town
Melbourne   Auckland

and associates in
Beirut   Berlin   Ibadan   Mexico City   Nicosia

Oxford is a trade mark of Oxford University Press

British Library Cataloguing in Publication Data

Other people's Clerihews
1. English wit and humour
I. Ewart, Gavin
821'.912   PN6175
ISBN 0-19-212982-1

Library of Congress Cataloging in Publication Data

Main entry under title:
Other people's clerihews
Includes index.
1. Clerihews.   2. Humorous poetry, English.
3. Biography – Poetry.   I. Ewart, Gavin.   II. Jennings, Nicola.
PR1195.C53084   1983   821'.07   82-24521

ISBN 0-19-212982-1

Typeset by Oxprint Ltd
Printed in Great Britain by
The Thetford Press Ltd,
Thetford, Norfolk

Contents

Introduction

THE title of this work, a collection of clerihews by authors other than Edmund Clerihew Bentley himself (who invented them in the early 1890s), presented problems. It was originally the intention to call it *Other Men's Clerihews*, echoing the title of Field Marshal Wavell's wartime verse anthology *Other Men's Flowers*. This was finally discarded, as being unfair to women – who have written some of the best contemporary clerihews. *Other People's Clerihews*, besides avoiding any hint of sexism, has also the merit of reminding those old enough to remember it of A. P. Herbert's song about nannies in a Thirties revue, 'Other People's Babies', very popular in its day.

In fact, long before Bentley arrived on the scene, the clerihew existed (like some rare flower awaiting classification by the botanist, or one of those accidentally discovered substances such as polythene) in the letters of Jane Austen. In a letter to her sister Cassandra, she wrote, in April 1811: 'Oh! yes, I remember Miss Emma Plumbtree's *Local* consequence perfectly. –

> "I am in a Dilemma, for want of an Emma,"
> "Escaped from the Lips, of Henry Gipps." –'

If this is written out in two couplets it is certainly a clerihew, in form at least. *Chambers Dictionary* gives perhaps the best short definition: 'a jingle in two short couplets purporting to quintessentialise the life and character of some notable person'. Anthony Hecht and John Hollander (in *Jiggery-Pokery*, a collection of double dactyls) call it 'that sublime and perfect mode which does for the personal name what Lear's form of the limerick . . . does for the place-name or attribute'.

Everybody knows Bentley's best ones. His son Nicolas, who illustrated many of them, was himself in the same class, and his piece on Cecil B. de Mille is famous. Nicolas also wrote six-line clerihews, an interesting innovation (see pp. 95–6).

The rhythms of prose are acceptable, and even desirable, as in the work of E. J. Thribb (17). The Ogden Nash rhyme does no harm, though it shouldn't be overdone:

> Girls shed their drawers
> To rawers of applawers
> But men look ridickerless
> Knickerless.

Perhaps this (by R. McGrail) does overdo it. It's a matter of opinion. Bentley never went in, much, for the mono-rhyme cleri-hew. Only two examples by him are known. But it can succeed:

> Graham Greene
> Has always been
> Very keen
> On dentists, death, and the childhood scene.
>
> *Maisie Archibald*

Bentley also thought that no clerihew should simply describe a historical fact; he never approved of his own brilliant piece to the effect that Louis Quatorze had a penchant for wars, and sent Turenne to the Palatinate, with instructions to flatten it. The fine rhyme is the beauty of this one. But rules are made to be broken.

> Though you may fill a mansion
> With volumes on scansion –
> If you draw a line for a poet
> Can you get him to toe it?
>
> *Ben Davies*

I have called the classical clerihew 'both civilised and dotty'; but there is no reason why sharp comment or lubricity should be avoided, if the writer feels like it. In an attempt to widen the scope, I have selected a few that are quite rumbustious, and some written with an edge of malice that Bentley would never have used; but I would never want or expect the clerihew to take over the rough and ready jollity of some limericks. On the other hand, clerihews are written for sophisticated people, and not for puritanical simpletons.

When I wrote the Introduction to *The Complete Clerihews of E. Clerihew Bentley* in 1980, I ventured the opinion that nobody except Bentley ever wrote really good clerihews. This opinion, in the face of the great number of fine ones that I've unearthed since I started preparing this book (with a lot of help from learnèd correspondents), I now withdraw. I am also certain that there are still many examples from magazine competitions which have escaped me. The Atlantic Ocean, too, I suspect, has separated me from beautiful and interesting work. I should be very grateful for any specimens that can be tracked down, in either case.

Clerihews can be of all ages and classes. In a recent *Sunday Times* competition two very accomplished entries came from children:

> Margaret Thatcher
> Sat in the house and tried to hatch a
> Plan to win her Cabinet's approval
> Before her removal.
>
> *Tom Smith (age* 11)

> Paul Michael Glazer
> Shaves his face with a razor.
> He shaves off a spot –
> But that's not the only one he's got.
>
> *Rebecca Dickinson (age* 12¾)

The final section of this book is devoted to sequences and mavericks of various sorts, including Nicolas Bentley's six-liners, referred to above. Sequences, in my opinion, are a very fruitful development. If every literary person in the British Isles could be persuaded to write a series of satirical clerihews about his or her personal literary enemies, literature would be greatly enriched – and some libel lawyers too, perhaps. Double dactyls, first cousins to clerihews, have been omitted, though they have a lot in common:

1066

Higgledy-piggledy
William the Conqueror
Landed at Pevensey,
Solid and sly,

Thickened the native tongue
Polysyllabically,
Gave to the monarchy
One in the eye.

Christopher Wallace-Crabbe

Some subjects seem to attract clerihews – Proust, Edward Heath, the Sitwells (several with rhymes for Sacheverell), Henry VIII, George MacBeth, Marie Antoinette, Gertrude Stein, the Borgias, Queen Victoria, Scott Fitzgerald, Sibelius (often in combination with Delius), Benjamin Britten, Nostradamus, for example. Each of these could claim two or more. Margaret Thatcher, Bernard Levin and Tony Benn were very popular in the *Sunday Times* contest. Yet good ones concerning these three were hard to find – about the last in particular, since the final word was said by Bentley himself (one might think) in his clerihew on Benn's father:

Of all sad words of tongue or pen
The saddest are Captain Wedgwood Benn,
Who, waving aloft his gory sabre,
Placed it at the disposal of Labour.

I jettisoned some quite good work in cases where the subjects were very much celebrities of the day and are now no longer widely known. This is always a danger when clerihews are topical, and some of the competition pieces of thirty or forty years ago (and more) run the risk that nobody now knows much, or anything, about the protagonists. Likewise, today's newscasters and pop stars may not be remembered tomorrow. Historical characters, for this reason, are always the safest to write about. I have also omitted all the very early clerihews by Bentley's schoolfriends; theirs may be found in *The First Clerihews*, published by Oxford University Press in facsimile in 1982.

The multiple clerihews about the same subject posed a problem. I didn't want to throw out a good one because I already had (what might be thought) a better one. On the other hand, two or three on the same subject must necessarily invite comparison, one with another, when the general arrangement – except for series and mavericks – is alphabetical. I can only hope that there is sufficient disagreement about merit among my readers to justify my procedure.

Specialists enjoy specialist clerihews. Philosophers like philosophical ones, musicians musical ones, and so on. The best ones, perhaps, should appeal to everybody with some culture or general knowledge. Many people don't like clerihews at all. One man's meat is another man's poison. I think myself that the lack of them (in Dr Johnson's sonorous phrases) would tend to eclipse the gaiety of nations and impoverish the public stock of harmless pleasure.

Naturally, in a book of this sort, overwhelming thanks are due to the many contributors and correspondents – too many to be listed individually – and also to Miss Nicola Jennings, whose illustrations are as it were the garnish on a tasty dish for the epicure of clerihews, as well as being admirable in their own right.

·ALPHABETICAL·

THESE clerihews are arranged in alphabetical order, according to the first letter of the most important name. For example, F. Scott Fitzgerald will appear under *F*, Little Bo-Peep under *L*, and Publius Ovidius Naso under *O* (Ovid). Footnotes are numbered according to the order of the clerihews on the page, to avoid disfiguring the verses with cues: so, for example, a note numbered 2 refers to the second clerihew on the page in question.

★

Henry Adams
Was mortally afraid of Madams:
In a disorderly house
He sat quiet as a mouse.

W. H. Auden

Agamemnon didn't see the writing on the wall
(Bear in mind, he wasn't very tall),
Viz. 'Vengeance is a'ter yer
Because of your ἁμαρτία.'

Paul Edwards

If I had been
Albertine
I'd have *disparue*
Too.

Ronald Mason

L. E. G. Ames
Was good at all games
But when batting at cricket
He was always L.E.G. before wicket.

James Moss

---

1 Henry Adams (1838–1918) came from the famous
Boston family that provided more than one President. He is
best known for an outstanding autobiography and his *History
of the United States*.

2 'Hamartia': sin or offence, the fatal flaw that is to be
found in all tragic characters.

3

One of Henry's peeves
Was that Anne of Cleves
Was cold
To hold.

J. C. Walker

Guillaume Apollinaire
Was seduced by an admirer from Beaucaire.
She didn't know she was too late
To be mentioned in the *Poésies complètes*.

John Adlard

The Arabian Nights
Give you fictional delights.
The Arabian Nations
Give you real palpitations.

Mark Adlard

Ares
Would play with the nymphs and fairies
And drive them about in fast cars
And buy them Mars bars.

Madge Knell

Anne of Cleves
Wore long, pointy sleeves.
They must have been a worry
When she ate curry.

Sylvia Haymon

5

Andy Pandy
Gets well away on brandy,
But Little Weed
Gets stoned on mead.

John Colmans

The historian Ausonius
Was totally erroneous
In believing that the Gauls
Had two pairs of balls.

J. D. K. Lloyd

The Emperor Aurelian
Was an intellectual chameleon.
His testamentary *non sequiturs*
Bewildered his executors.

Anon.

The Ayatollah
Is a fella you have to follah
If you want to live your allotted span
In Iran.

J. M. L. Harris

Johann Sebastian Bach,
When a cello string went, would say 'Ach!'
(So says our reliable source).
A gut reaction, of course.

Paul Bridle

But for Logie Baird
That good old Yogi Bear'd
Never have been seen
On your television screen.

Anon.

I'm glad they called Baldwin Stanley.
It sounds so manly.
What a mercy
They didn't christen him Percy.

Anon.

Baudelaire
Said 'I do not care:
I *shall*
Write *Les Fleurs du mal*'.

R. A. Maitre

'Now, this', said the Venerable Bede,
'Is a very important matter indeed:
Would it be uncanonical
To contribute to the *Anglo-Saxon Chronicle?*'

B. G. Smallman

Mrs Belloc-Lowndes
Never gave grounds
For excessive admiration
Of her ratiocination.

Jacques Barzun

Jeremy Bentham,
When they played the National Anthem,
Sat on,
With his hat on.

John Whitworth

. . . and incidentally,
Mr Bentley,
Will someone write a clerihew
When they bury you?

R. H. Sampson

Isaiah Berlin
Stood on the head of a pin
(Displacing numberless angels without apology)
And gave a lecture on epistemology.

Henry Hardy

1 Mrs Belloc-Lowndes (1868–1947), sister of Hilaire Belloc, was a successful popular novelist.

3 John Nevinson writes: 'I recall hearing the last words of a speech, when E.C.B. was entertained by the Detection Club, and [Bentley] was greatly annoyed when Major R. H. Sampson ('Richard Hull', the writer of detective stories) concluded . . . [as above].'

Biography
Is different from musicography:
Biography is about fellows,
Musicography is about cellos.

Anon.

In spite of the significance and all that
Of the cardinal's hat,
I like the biretta
Better.

Elizabeth Lister

William Blake
Kept a spotted snake,
But Cardinal Newman
Kept a spotted woman.

James Elroy Flecker

William Blake
Found Newton hard to take,
And was not enormously taken
With Francis Bacon.

W. H. Auden

Boadicea
Was rather a dear.
She drove about with great abandon
And left her critics without a leg to stand on.

Bill Belcher

Rodrigo Borgia,
A frequent orgier,
Said 'I fill the Vatican
With all the whores that I can!'

F. Pitt-Kethley

John Wilkes Booth
(And this is the truth)
Shares much of the blame
For Theater's bad name.

Louis Phillips

Botticelli
Loved botti and belli
And faces that thin
To a porcelain chin.

I. D. M. Morley

While conducting the '1812' Pierre Boulez
Was shot in the goulez.
He should have sat on
His baton.

Derrick Carter

Sir Donald Bradman
Would have been a very glad man
If his Test average had been .06 more
Than 99.94.

T. N. E. Smith

Brahms and Liszt
Were frequently pissed,
Though biographies do not say whether
They were ever pissed together.

F. Pitt-Kethley

Bramante
Had a dear old auntie
Who made his rooms in Rome
A Home from Home.

Giles Robertson

Benjamin Britten
Said his operas were only written
For Peter Pears to sing
Because he couldn't get Bing.

P. Macnamara

Has Benjamin Britten
Over-written?
Not to the ears
Of Peter Pears.

Anon.

Emily Brontë
Became rather jaunty
When Wuthering Heights
Became one of the tourist sites.

Joan Littlejohn

Emily Brontë
Took her crayons by Conté
And drew pricks, cunts and balls
On the Parsonage walls.

F. Pitt-Kethley

Rupert Brooke
Sure did look
Pale, beautiful and good
As young poets should.

Wendy Cope

Robert Browning
Was always frowning,
Which made Elizabeth Barrett
As sick as a parrot.

David Lilley

Robert Bruce
Was going to call a truce,
When he saw an arachnid . . .
And the rest of the story's hackneyed.

M. M. Buchanan

Isambard Kingdom Brunel
Gave off a peculiar smell
Which he donated to the nation
And it's still there in Paddington Station.

Edwin Loveday

Michelangelo Buonarroti
Used to go to Chapel quite a lot: he
Said 'I have a feeling
I could improve that ceiling!'

A. M. Chapman

Doctor Guy Burniston Brown,
An astrophysicist of renown,
Has shown by every argument pennable
That Einstein's Special Theory is untenable.

Mark Haimon

One often yearns
For the land of Burns –
The only snag is
The haggis!

Lils Emslie

Robert Burton
Fornicated with a girl from Girton.
He found her anatomy jolly
And it took his mind off melancholy.

R. A. Maitre

I think Bustamante
Is better than Dante.
Dante had to go down to Hell.
Bustamante can raise the place quite well!

Anon.

If R. A. Butler
Had been subtler
He might have been home and dry – it made him
    fume
When the Prime Minister was dry and Home.

Elsie Miller

Dame Clara Butt
Packed a lethal upper-cut;
So, when it appeared that she could also sing,
She began her career in *The Ring*.

L. N. Button

George Gordon, Lord Byron,
Never had the fire on –
He slept warm with a Great Dane, a cockatoo
And a mistress or two.

Joyce Sugg

Caligula sent Incitatus
To the Senatus.
Other parts of horses have also been sent
To Parliament.

R. V. Burns and D. Jon Grossman

Canova
May be distinguished from Casanova.
Though both attempted the nude,
Canova was less rude.

Felix Aylmer

The Archbishop of Canterbury
Said the Dean was the man to bury:
'Will no one, West or East,
Rid me of this turbulent priest?'

J. M. Ross

4 The Archbishop is Geoffrey Fisher, when Dr Hewlett
Johnson was Dean ('The Red Dean').

The Reverend Charles Dodgson, alias Lewis Carroll,
One day opened his apparel
To show a little girl named Alice
His phallus.

Paul Curry Steele

Thomas Carlyle
Was once observed to smile.
He married Jane
And it didn't happen again.

John Whitworth

Geoffrey Chaucer
Always drank out of a saucer.
He said it made him feel such an ass
To drink out of a glass.

Anon.

Cimabue
Liked his food gooey.
Giotto
Preferred a plain risotto.

Giles Robertson

When Arthur Hugh Clough
Was jilted by a piece of fluff,
He sighed 'Quel dommage!',
And wrote *Amours de voyage*.

W. H. Auden

William Cobbett
Never discovered a hobbit,
Although he tried
On every Rural Ride.

Robin Skelton

Roy Cohn
Has a head like a bone
Upon which are features
To give you the screechers.

William Cole

S. Connery as 007
Was most women's idea of heaven –
I too would him adore,
Loved I not Roger Moore.

Jean Husband

Ms Jilly Cooper
Is jolly super.
She looks through rose-coloured glasses
At the middle classes.

Carol Chisholm

Many plays
Of Corneille's
Are about folks
Who can't take jokes.

Sarah Lawson

Fanny Craddock
Couldn't endure haddock
Even *un tout petit peu* –
Unless it was cordon bleu.

Gavin Ewart

Crébillon Fils
Didn't write books like *War and Peace*.
For him, a war was a non-event;
He preferred spanking in a conevent.

Gavin Ewart

Quentin Crisp
Speaks with a lisp.
He is not ineffectual
At championing the homosexual.

Carol Chisholm

Mr Crotch and Mr Pratt
Would like you to remember that
They were the two young Cambridge men
Who wrote the tune chimed by Big Ben.

Dorothy Jewell

Cynewulf
May have been digested *in* a wolf
Or he may have been killed by a foreigner –
We have no report from a coroner.

Richard Leighton Greene

Salvador Dali
Was a bit of a charlie,
And polite Japanese say 'Ah, so'
To Picasso.

J. Glasgow

Salvador Dali
Se fichait du vulgaire hallali.
Afin de ne pas entendre
Il s'est coiffé d'un scaphandre.

M. M.

2 Cynewulf is one of the few Anglo-Saxon poets of the early
ninth century whose name is known, and that only because he
built it into his verses with runes.

4 'Salvador Dali was fed up with vulgar whoops and cries.
So as not to hear them, he put a diver's helmet on his head.'

General de Gaulle
Was always playing a role,
And went about in a trance,
Convinced that he was France.

Alastair Smart

25

Joan
Although she was known
As 'd'Arc', had fair
Hair.

S. Todd

President Charles de Gaulle
Staked his future on the poll
And having polled more *nons* than *ouis*
Went home to Colombey-les-deux-Églises.

John Pinnell

Cecil B. de Mille,
Rather against his will,
Was persuaded to leave Moses
Out of *The Wars of the Roses*.

Nicolas Bentley

Alfred de Musset
Used to call his cat Pusset.
His accent was affected.
That was to be expected.

Maurice Hare

Debenham & Freebody
Each had a wee body,
And it comes as a surprise
That their parents were of normal size.

Nicolas Bentley

The music of Delius
Appeals to the supercelius
Who consider that Elgar
Is velgar.

E. L. Mascall

Those who don't think Delius
Simply marvelius
Should take a dose of Beecham:
That'll teach 'em.

Edmond Kapp

Descartes had a clear
And distinct idea
Of what Bishop Berkeley
Saw through a glass darkly.

John Sparrow

DELIVERANCE

Never read James Dickey
when the weather's hot and icky.

The time for dickey-dunkin
's when the frost is on the punkin.

Jonathan Williams

Though Diefenbaker
Was a faker,
He was not as pseudo
As Trudeau.

D. E. Tacium

Diodorus Siculus
Rendered himself ridiculous
By asserting that thimbles
Were phallic symbols.

C. D. Broad

As a youth, John Donne
Had a lot of fun.
After he hung up his balls,
He became Dean of St Paul's.

Ivan Berger

Diogenes
Wasn't hard to please:
His sole apparel
Was a barrel.

B. G. Smallman

Margaret Drabble
Isn't read by the rabble,
Though popular enough.
They prefer Cartland's stuff.

Sarah Lawson

Edwin Drood
Has led too many to brood;
In their endings the plot needlessly thickens.
I wish they would go to the Dickens.

Jacques Barzun

Isadora Duncan
Said airily 'Anyone can
Dance if they take off their shoes.
And why bother with frou-frous?'

Carol Rumens

Albrecht Dürer
Naturally never heard of the Führer.
I wonder if the latter . . .
But that doesn't really matter.

W. Leslie Nicholls

I wonder if Ecclesiastes
Could have been cheered up by a glass of pastis,
And if a double brandy
Might even have made him feel randy.

Carol Rumens

Albert Einstein declared
That $E = mc^2$
But relatively few
Can prove that it's true.

John W. A. Roberts

The celebrated Dr Einstein
Blew the rising foam off a fine stein
Of beer and said with suavity:
What a nice antidote to gravity!

Palmer Bovie

Eisenhower
Wielded a great deal of power.
His lady chauffeur drove his motor with pride
And gave him a jolly good ride.

William Sherwood

Eleanor of Aquitaine
Could be a bit of a pain,
Or so King Henry II
Reckoned.

R. J. A. Fox

So many people thought Domenico Theotocopouli
A name unduly unruly that they decided quite
  coolly:
'Ecco! –
El Greco!'

Edmond Kapp

F. Scott Fitzgerald
Was nattily apparelled;
He was married to a flapper
Who was likewise very dapper.

Richard Leighton Greene

Scott and Zelda
Always held a
Brief for sports
Who soaked-up shorts.

C. E. Harrold

L'Avenue Foch
Is for people who are posh:
L'Avenue Victor Hugo
Is where people like me and you go.

Charles Hennessy

Jane Fonda
Was often inclined to ponder
On the state of the Western nations,
If they continued to ignore her anti-nuclear
  demonstrations.

C. W. Carson

John Fowles
Prefers owls
And zen   .
To media men.

Anthony Curtis

Will Francis of Assisi
Still sleep easy –
Called, in mediaparaphraseology,
'The Patron Saint of Ecology'?

Lorna Davies

4 This title was used in *Radio Times*, October 1981.

The prose of Lady Antonia Fraser
Cuts like a razor.
Pinter
Is more of a hinter.

Anthony Curtis

Sigmund Freud
Thought no man could avoid
Wanting a bit of the other
With his mother.

R. A. Maitre

Drink,
Opined Elisabeth Frink,
Never helps me to draw.
But with sculpture I always say 'Oh, yes, please,
    Henry, more!'

David Hughes

Robert Frost
Counted the cost
Of uxoricide:
It cost a lot so he let it slide.

D. E. Tacium

If Fuseli
Had invented Muesli
We'd have to re-chart
The history of art.

Jeremy Adler

Genghis Khan
Wintered in Afghanistan.
When the weather was finer
He moved into China.

M. J. Shepherd

Please do not mention
The gentian.
It is too
Blue.

Anon.

Mihail Glinka
Was a perfect stinker.
He told Ippolitov-Ivanov, 'Only wretches
Will applaud your *Causasian Sketches.*'

D. Jon Grossman

Lady Godiva
Said 'I'll do it for a fiver,
Providing, of course,
That you blindfold the horse.'

Cecil Hardy

'Not again for a fiver!'
Confessed Lady Godiva.
'You'd never believe how much a horse itches
When you're not wearing breeches!'

Livingstone K. Bluntnose

Johann Wolfgang Goethe
Did not write *Die Zauberflöte*,
As every cultured person knows.
Goethe wrote oratorios.

Paul Curry Steele

Johann Wolfgang Goethe
Spielte gerne Flöte.
Sein Freund Schiller
Spielte lieber Triller.

F. Kaminski

4 'Johann Wolfgang Goethe liked playing the flute. His friend Schiller preferred playing trills.'

Rubber corsets are able
To give you a figure like Betty Grable:
But afterwards from behind
You look like something written for the blind.

Anon.

The family of Goossens
Found it a nuisance
When a Goossens was born with no real
Talent for anything but the glockenspiel.

V. H. Porter

W. G. Grace
Hated losing face,
So under his whiskers
He planted hibiscus.

Alan Ross

Lord Grade
Is entirely self-made.
You may love him or hate him
But-if-he-didn't-exist-would-we-have-to-create-
him?

Alan Clark

Percy Aldridge Grainger
Preferred to live with danger;
But his activities had to be banned
When he produced his *Handel in the Strand*.

L. N. Button

4 The Strand was the place for pick-ups in Victorian and
even later times. It could have been described as a good place
for 'handling' people.

Through country churchyards Thomas Gray
Plodded his weary way,
Only stopping to moan a
Faint *Floreat Etona!*

Georgina Hammick

I always think of Greek
Women as noble, antique
And practically nude
Except for a snood.

Harold Booth

Fulke Greville
Wrote beautifully at sea-level:
With each rising contour his verse
Got progressively worse.

W. H. Auden

Lady Jane Grey's
Reign lasted nine days.
Never flaunt
The fact that you descend from John of Gaunt.

D. Jon Grossman

Sir George Grove
Was quite a versatile cove.
He was the only lighthouse-designer
Ever to write a Mass in B minor.

L. N. Button

Countess Guiccioli
Remarked, rather bitchily,
That Byron
Was not made of iron.

Daryl Hine

Queen Guinevere
Would have liked a career
But Arthur and Lancelot
Were what she got.

Wendy Cope

Gurdjieff
Was partially deaf.
He had to wear a card on
His chest, saying PARDON?

Robert Calvert

Who will recall,
Say, Henry Hall
When, say, Billy Cotton
Is forgotten?

Edmond Kapp

It is unfair
To be too hard on Hare;
Early anatomical work
Owes much to men like him and Burke.

Anon.

Jean C. Harris,
Paying her first visit to Paris
And thinking of Edouard Manet,
Cried, 'Now is the time to *flâner!*

Mark Roskill

Seamus Heaney
Is such a meany
He puts all his pomes
In extremely slim tomes.

Angus O'Hara

3 Jean C. Harris, art historian and authoress of *Edouard Manet, Graphic Works: A Definitive Catalogue* (New York, 1970). Manet's *Concert in the Tuileries* includes the artist himself in the picture, in the role of *flâneur* (stroller of the boulevards and observer). From this derives the term '*flâneur* realism' for this phase of his art.

All
We shall recall
Of Edward Heath
Is teeth.

Edmond Kapp

There may be nothing finer
Than the poetry of Heine,
But the news that Mr Upton Sinclair,
   Sir Rabindranath Tagore and Mr John
   Galsworthy are on a committee formed to
   discuss the erection of a memorial on his behalf
Makes me laugh.

J. B. Morton

Henry VIII avoided bigamy
By a system of serial polygamy.
When his fancy ranged
He just chopped and changed.

David Baxandall

Henry Eight
Got up late.
Perhaps there was something to be said
For *his* staying in bed.

Edmond Kapp

Heptonstall
Is interesting, but small;
If you want crumpets or fish and chips or woolly
   socks or medicated hair shampoo or non-stick
   saucepans or an electric cooker or a fridge,
Choose Hebden Bridge.

Ruth Silcock

Houdini
Was teeny.
No one could bind him –
They couldn't even find him.

Ruth Silcock

Can you enthuse
About Ted Hughes
If you don't know
A wren from a crow?

Wendy Cope

Mr Spike Hughes,
An authority on the Blues,
Has also declared he
Is simply nuts about Verdi.

Bernard Bergonzi

David Hume,
Whenever attacked by gloom
At the thought of substance or causation,
Played backgammon with marked exhilaration.

J. C. Maxwell

If
Bores me stiff –
Particularly when framed and hung on the wall
In a palatial hall.

Granville Garley

Dean Inge
Went out on a binge.
He had a great many falls
On the way back to St Paul's.

Spike Hughes

The performances of Sir Henry Irving
Were occasionally unnerving.
His sudden cry of 'Anyone for tennis?'
Was quite exceptional, even in Act II of
The Merchant of Venice.

Martin Knapp

Clive James
Knows lots of names
Of foreign writers.
He can even pronounce Heraclitus.

Carol Rumens

Clive James
Had some Royal fun with names.
To flatter or sting? It was a bind.
He couldn't do both – or make up his mind.

Peter McGivern

JACOBEAN

Henry James
(Whatever his other claims)
Is not always too deuced
Lucid.

Clifton Fadiman

Jerome K. Jerome
Would ask anyone home
If he found they could quote
From *Three Men in a Boat*.

Joanne Hill

Was Jesus
Sent to please us?
Or simply to soft-sell
Hell?

R. A. Maitre

When Augustus John
Really does stick it on
His price is within about 4d.
Of Orpen's.

Edmond Kapp

James Joyce
Lived abroad for choice.
The same is
Apparently not true of Kingsley Amis.

John Adlard

Anna Karenina
Had a pain in her
Soul. The pain
Was cured by a train.

David Baxandall

Paul Klee
Made hay
Of Romney
Et hoc genus omne.

John Gilmour

1 For those unfamiliar with the old currency,
4d = fourpence.

PARASITES LOST

'Twas at Verona that Keats,
Finding strange company between the sheets,
To obviate the necessity of further meetings
Invented Keatings.

Edmond Kapp

1 Keatings Powder was for many years in Victorian
and Edwardian times the specific destroyer of fleas.

48

Nikita Krushchev
Took one of his shoes off.
He said' '*We* invented the clerihew
And, what's more, we will berihew.'

Pyke Johnson Jr

Alan Ladd
Wasn't half bad:
Indeed, standing on a block of wood,
He was more than half-good.

Bill Greenwell

Lady Caroline Lamb
Was a *fatale* sort of *femme*,
The things she did to poor Lord Melbourne
Were shocking in one so well born.

M. R. Jolly

Sir Lancelot
Used to dance a lot;
None of the dancers
Excelled him in The Lancers.

John Sparrow

1 Krushchev, the Soviet Prime Minister (1958–64), made a
speech in September 1959 in which he said, if the West should
attack, 'we will bury you'.

Mr D. H. Lawrence
Went to live in Florence.
If it had been Mr Compton Mackenzie
He would have called it Firenze.

Anon.

Don't talk to me
About D.H. and T.E.
The Lawrences
Are my abhorrences.

Anon.

In politer days
'Good lays'
Were ditties –
Not pretties.

Hardy Amies

Laurie Lee
Can get grumpy on tea
But on cider (with Rosie)
He's cuddly and cosy.

Georgina Hammick

Doris Lessing
Doesn't keep you guessing;
The volumes come thicker and faster
And stretch from here to Shikasta.

Sarah Lawson

Bernard Levin
Reckoned his idea of Heaven
Would be hearing *The Ring* ring through the
   spheres,
And going on for ever, instead of just for years.

Paul Bridle

Lillee
c. Dilley
b.
Old.

John Pinnell

Fra Filippo Lippi
Was neat and nippy
When it was a question of coming between
   Lucrezia Buti
And her duty.

Giles Robertson

Little Bo-Peep
Has lost her sleep
Showing Little Boy Blue
What to do.

R. J. Jacques

Christopher Logue
Is writing for *Vogue:*
This has got Doris Lessing
Guessing . . .

Kenneth Tynan

Percival Lowell,
Wise as an owl,
Thought sister Amy
A little bit gamey.

Louis Phillips

Luther & Zwingli
Should be treated singly:
L. hated the Peasants,
Z. the Real Presence.

W. H. Auden

3 Amy Lowell (1874–1925) was a noted American poet, of a romantic kind.

George MacBeth
Paused a moment for breath
And fourteen ladies in black leather
Chased him across the heather.

Fleur Adcock

George MacBeth
Wrote poems about death.
At least, that's what I *think* they are about:
Their meanings leave a considerable amount of
   room for doubt.

Fred Sedgwick

One must believe,
With Hugh MacDiarmid (Christopher Murray
   Grieve),
There will always be a Scotland. Whatever's the
   o'clock,
There's teuch sauchs growin' i' the Reuch Heuch
   Hauch.

Clark Emery

Niccolò Machiavelli
Had a cast-iron belly;
He thought dinners with the Borgias
Were gorgeous.

Terence Tiller

3 The last line means 'There are tough willows growing in
the Reuch Heuch Hauch [a field near Hawick, a town in
south-east Scotland]'.

The fans of Norman Mailer
Outnumber those of Vlad the Impaler.
I suppose people would rather be mailed
Than impaled.

Bob Knowles

Marie Antoinette
Was most upset
By the French Revolution:
It ruined her elocution.

Ruth Silcock

Charles Gustavus Markbreiter
Thought hard about making Sark brighter,
But left the scheme on the shelf,
Murmuring 'What about myself?'

J. M. Ross

Martial
Was sexually impartial
But *everybody* swung both ways
In the old Roman days.

John Whitworth

3 Markbreiter was head of the division of the Civil Service
concerned with the Channel Islands in the 1930s.

Marie Antoinette's mistake
Was to say 'Let them eat cake!'
Though it sounded much more posh
As 'Qu'ils mangent de la brioche!'

Lils Emslie

Marx, Dada and Spooner
Are remembered sooner
Not for being mentally lissom,
But for having discovered an 'ism'.

Ben Morgan

Massenet
Never wrote a Mass in A.
It'd have been just too bad,
If he had.

Anthony Butts

Maud
Said 'I've never been more bored:
My dear, I dragged outside to keep this tryst –
Where was he? In the flower bed, Brahms and
   Liszt!'

Connie Bensley

George Melly
Is often on the telly.
He talks about pictures and that
In a felt hat.

R. A. Maitre

The Mikado of Japan
Is an extraordinary man:
He lives in the tops of trees,
Surrounded by Japanese.

Edmond Kapp

To confuse Jean François Millet
With *our* John Millais is silly:
Millet was French, and had money troubles –
Quite unlike the painter of *Bubbles*.

T. Palmer

If A. A. Milne
Had fired a kiln,
He would have made lots
Of honey-pots.

Bill Greenwell

Mona Lisa
Set Leonardo a teaser,
And centuries later
Was still puzzling Walter Pater.

Anon.

Thomas Moore
Caused a furore
Every time he bellowed his
Irish Melodies.

W. H. Auden

A. J. Munnings, RA,
Knows all about hay;
But for an equestrian
His works are oddly pedestrian.

Towanbucket

Len Murray
Hated curry.
It didn't go well with T.
U.C.

J. Wallace

The Emperor Nero
Was not a Christian hero.
He used the communicants
As street illuminants.

Guy Barton

I like Norman naves.
One sits behind pillars and misbehaves.
One has to be more particular
In Perpendicular.

Anon.

Pious Miss Nevill
Was raped by a retromingent devil.
Experiences so prodigious
Are reserved for the morbidly religious.

John Adlard

Nietzsche
Used to note down every fietzsche
Of the human psyche.
Cryche!

Anon.

Anais Nin
Had a journal she wrote things in.
She seemed to need it,
But do we have to read it?

Robin Skelton

Nostradamus
Never wore pyjamas;
'What's the use,' he would say,
'When the world may not last the night anyway?'

J. A. Gammon

Nostradamus
Was famous
For his predictions in rhyme –
Wrong most of the time.

Mark Haimon

The author of *The Story of O*
Is not the kind of person feminists would care to
   know,
For girls can only figure as inferiors
If they let gentlemen whip their posteriors.

John Adlard

Oedipus Rex
Said 'My idea of sex
Is a bit of the other
With Mother.'

Charles Hennessy

Publius Ovidius Naso,
Tho' too much of a gentleman to say so,
Was banished because he saw Julia
Doing something peculiar.

B. G. Smallman

Palladio
Was a great success on the radio,
But his appearance on television
Was greeted with derision.

Giles Robertson

Mungo ('Finsbury') Park
Explored Africa when it was dark.
He later acknowledged a slight
Preference for the Isle of Wight.

L. N. Button

Louis Pasteur
Worked fasteur
Than others of his ilk
In purifying milk.

D. R. Gibbins

William Penn
Was the most level-headed of men;
He had only one mania –
Pennsylvania.

William Jay Smith

2 Finsbury Park is a not very artistocratic park in the north of London.

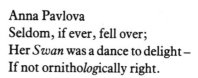

Anna Pavlova
Seldom, if ever, fell over;
Her *Swan* was a dance to delight –
If not ornitho*log*ically right.

Bernard D. Smith

Samuel Pepys
Said it gave him the creeps
To see Nell Gwynn beckoned
By Charles the Second.

Allan M. Laing

The Emperor Pertinax
Possessed a certain axe,
With which he used to strike
Those whom he did not like.

F. W. Haskins

Le maréchal Pétain
Etait amoureux de grands tétins.
C'était plutôt un masseur
Qu'un concasseur.

Terence Tiller

Petrarch
Had the mentality of a tetrarch.
He said, 'If they don't like my sonnets
They have bees in their bonnets.'

D. Jon Grossman

---

3 'Marshal Pétain was very fond of big tits. He was more a
stroker than a crusher.' Or, in the words of the poet himself:

It was to boopers that Marshal
Pétain was most partial:
He thought massage refineder
Than being a heavy grinder.

Philpotts, Eden
Is rural readin'
But murder done by or on a peasant
Is none the less pleasant.

Jacques Barzun

Colonel Ebenezer Pike,
By a coincidence most unlike-
ly, of which people still speak,
Discovered Pike's Peak.

Clark Stillman

The Pill
Won't cure every human ill,
But when you're randy
It comes in handy.

D. Jon Grossman

Harold Pinter
Never looks forward to winter:
Sex without cricket
Gets on his wicket.

Georgina Hammick

1 Eden Philpotts (1862–1960), author of at least 150
works, mainly concerning English rustic life, was famous for
his novels and for two plays, *The Farmer's Wife* and *Yellow
Sands* (written in collaboration with his daughter Adelaide
Philpotts).

William Pitt
Fell, on the 18th green, in an apoplectic fit.
All around enjoyed the joke
As Fox murmured 'Beaten, by a stroke!'

Anon.

Sylvia Plath
Liked to sing in the bath,
But you'd never know it –
She was that kind of poet.

Sarah Lawson

Roman Polanski
Is a very small manski –
So his taste in women'll
Always be criminal.

Joyce Nice

Alexander Pope
Had good reason to hope
That posterity would neither slander
Nor confuse him with Pope Alexander.

Willy Barth

Alexander Pope
Occasionally smoked old rope;
A feat which used to sicken 'em
In the neighbourhood of Twickenham.

H. A. Johnson

On top of Popocatepetl
Foreigners are in fine fetl;
They can either sit and titl-tatl
Or look across at Itaccihuatl.

Bill Greenwell

Pride and Prejudice has not
A complicated plot.
Snobbery subdued by Charm and Wit –
That's it.

F.C.C.

Said the great chemist Priestley,
'I'm feeling rather beastly.
My breathing is on the rocks again;
I think I'll discover oxygen.'

Clark Stillman

Proust
Used
To wear white gloves in bed:
Enough said.

J. G. Fairfax

Marcel Proust
Was forbidden to eat *langouste*
But would cruise the lowest bar
In search of *homard*.

John Hollander

When Marcel Proust
Came home to roost
He said 'There is no sadder lane
Than a madeleine.'

David Grantley

Emilio Pucci
Called his wife Gucci:
This wasn't just a gag –
She really was a bag.

Clifford Field

Henry Purcell
Was often drunk at rehearsal.
But, as he said, he thought it best
Always to start with a few bars' rest.

Desmond Bland

God was quite right
To say: 'Let there be light!' –
It's a much nicer remark
Than 'Let there be quark!'

C. E. Harrold

Redundancy pay
Is not a bad way
To learn at last
You're a thing of the past.

Reay Fuller

Romain Rolland
Wasn't taken seriously in Holland.
The Dutch even had the nerve
To try and canalise the *roman-fleuve*.

Carol Rumens

Dante Gabriel Rossetti
Had quantities and quantities of confetti,
Unlike poor Canaletto
Who only had one confetto.

Kate Bleckie

Dante Gabriel Rossetti
Hated spaghetti
Although he learned, albeit slowly,
To enjoy ravioli.

John Colmans

REFLECTIONS UPON THE NOBLE SAVAGE

The bride of Jean-Jacques Rousseau
Had a too-exiguous trousseau:
One cannot enter *le high-life*
In a mere fig-leaf.

Terence Tiller

Dr A. L. Rowse
Slept in Shakespeare's house.
There was a ghostly knock on the door,
And there stood the Second Part of Henry IV.

Roger Coombs

The brainchild of Professor Rubik
Is clearly cubic.
But other circles made the profit
That spun off it.

B. W. T. McGrath

The Bishop of St Albans
Preferred large buns to small buns.
'Nothing', he said, 'can be truly $\mathring{\alpha}\gamma\alpha\theta\grave{o}\varsigma$
Without a certain $\mu\acute{e}\gamma\epsilon\theta o\varsigma$!'

J. M. Ross

St Francis of Sales
Said 'I have converted the Prince of Wales.'
St Francis Xavier
Said 'Oh, yer 'ave, 'ave yer?'

Guy Barton

St Simeon Stylites
Held no brief for see-through nighties.
They simply were not in his line;
But at pillar-talk he was fine.

Paul Bridle

In the War, one didn't know
That Hector Hugh Munro
Was Saki
In khaki.

R. Lyons

---

[1] The Bishop in question is Philip Loyd. 'Agathos' means 'good', 'megethos' 'size', in Ancient Greek.

Salome
Wasn't what you'd call 'homey'.
Her dish for a feast
Was *Tête Baptiste*.

Joyce Johnson

Lou Salome tended to be bitchy
In her relations with Nietzsche
And others of his ilk
Including Freud and Rilke.

D. Jon Grossman

George Sand
Was always dropping her *gant*
For musicians and men of letters,
Mostly her youngers and betters.

Antonia Cowan

Sant' Apollinare in Classe
Is splendidly massy;
Any discerning juror
Would prefer it to San Paolo fuori le Mura.

David Baxandall

Sir Malcolm Sargent
Wore buttonholes – gules, or and argent –
They generated odium
Each time he mounted the podium.

Gavin Ewart

When Jean-Paul Sartre visited London
He left his fly-buttons undone,
Saying 'I don't care what your laws are –
I intend to *épater les bourgeois*.'

Gerald Priestland

When Dorothy Sayers
Went to dine at the Lord Mayor's,
He cried 'Sapristi!
Where's Agatha Christie?'

D. Jon Grossman

What used to make Schopenhauer
Cower
With fear
Was that his mum had more will than idea.

Jeremy Adler

74

Franz Schubert
Trug den Hut umgekehrt;
Dazu, was ist noch besser,
Frass Erbsen mit dem Messer.

E. J. Evans

Cyril Scott
Like German, is not:
But Britten
Is almost as written.

M. Cassel

There is a terrible lot
Of Sir Walter Scott.
As a rule
You read one or two at school.

John Letts

G.B.S.
Said 'The world's in a mess.
Plainly the cause
Is the shortage of Shaws.'

G. C. B. Andrew

---

[1] 'Franz Schubert wore his hat the wrong way round. And in addition, which is even better, he ate peas with a knife.'

Mrs Shilling
(Herself quite thrilling)
Drives fetishists bats
With her kinky hats.

George Moor

The symphonies of Sibelius
Were all financial failures;
Quite unlike Mahler's,
Which raked in the dollars.

Gerald Priestland

Dame Edith Sitwell
I didn't like a bit well;
But her enthusiasms were several –
Sir Osbert and Sacheverell.

William Cole

Edith and Sacheverell Sitwell –
Say it quick and spit well.
Pause and say it slow
Or your Freudian slip will show.

Greg Wren

Edith and Osbert Sitwell
Had hats that didn't fit well;
So they borrowed several
From Sacheverell.

Anon.

I must not mock
Dr Spock
But I wish someone or other could
Tell me how a man became an expert on
  motherhood.

Olive Howard

Dame Freya Stark
Never walks in the Park;
She prefers to cure inertia
By walking over Persia.

R. J. Jacques

Gertrude Stein
Is famous for just one line.
Now everyone knows
That a rose is a rose is a rose.

V. Gibberd

LES MATINS DANS LA RUE FLEURUS NO 27

Gertrude Stein
arose at nine

and arose and arose
and arose

Jonathan Williams

Laurence Sterne
Liked French chambermaids, if they were *jeunes*.
To get to know them better
He would send them a French letter.

Gavin Ewart

4 A French letter is called by the French *capote anglaise*.

Marie Stopes
Raised people's hopes
That copulation
Would not result in increased population.

Helen MacGregor

Johann Strauss
Had so little nous
He believed it was true
That the Danube is blue.

Alan Clark

A bottle or two of Strega
Makes conversation vaguer;
But many a party takes leave of its
Senses, on slivovitz.

Terence Tiller

Jonathan Swift
Never went up in a lift;
Nor did the author of *Robinson Crusoe*
Do so.

Edmond Kapp

Poor Algernon Swinburne,
The birches of Eton made his skin burn,
But his problems were understood
By certain ladies in St John's Wood.

John Adlard

'KENNST DU DAS LAND . . .'

John Addington Symonds
was very fond of lemons,

plucked by Venetian gondoliers
graced with jolly great big ears

Jonathan Williams

Rabindranath Tagore
Made flowers bloom where there were none
    before.
'It's my green thumb,' he said, 'and with my tan
    thumb
I do stuff like the Indian National Anthem.'

George Starbuck

Georg Philipp Telemann
Wasn't a 'Hello, sailor!' man.
He was fond of girls, in his own fashion,
And wrote over forty settings of the Passion.

Gavin Ewart

William Tell
Shot apples as they fell;
He considered it unfitting
When invited to shoot one sitting.

Anon.

Lord Tennyson
Dined frequently on venison.
When asked if this was cheap, he said: 'No fear!
It's deer.'

Yvonne Kapp

Tetrazzini
Was a regular meanie;
She shouted 'To Elba
With Melba!'

Anthony Butts

William Makepeace Thackeray
Was a lifetime collector of knick-knackery.
He left Oliver Wendell Holmes
Two gnomes.

Frank Muir

Monsieur Toulouse-Lautrec,
When pressed to honour a cheque,
Said 'Can't I have two weeks, or three?
I'm a bit short at present, you see!'

Bernard D. Smith

83

Violet Trefusis went quite loco
If offered bedtime cocoa.
She could sleep sweeter
With Vita.

Georgina Hammick

Dylan Thomas
Has passed from us.
But *Under Milk Wood*
Is still quite good.

> *R. A. Maitre*

Anthony Thwaite
Found he was losing weight
Keeping up the pecker
Of Secker.

> *Fleur Adcock*

J. R. R. Tolkien
Was not, on the whole, keen
On trolls made of plastic,
But he thought gnomes were fantastic.

> *Joanne Hill*

Whereas Trinity Sunday
Is just *one* day,
The Sundays *after* Trinity
Seem to stretch to infinity.

> *Leslie Johnson*

2 Anthony Thwaite, noted British poet, critic and editor,
selects the poetry published by Secker & Warburg.

Dick Turpin
Was bent as a hairpin,
And Black Bess his nag
Was a stallion in drag.

John Whitworth

King Tut
Would have preferred to remain shut,
Being in no condition
To go on exhibition.

Paul Maher

S. S. Van Dine
Had cause to repine:
He was the only man who ever
Thought Philo Vance was clever.

Jacques Barzun

Sir Anthony van Dyck
Was the sort of painter I like.
Almost anything he did
Is worth several quid.

Sir Thomas Bodkin

P. Vergilius Maro
Was not educated at Harrow
But at home –
i.e. Rome.

A. I. F. Mackenzie

Queen Victoria
Never went to the Astoria
To see *Deep Throat*.
She didn't even have the vote.

Carol Rumens

When Baron von Hügel
Came to church with a bügel
The Abbé Loisy
Asked him not to be so noisy.

E. L. Mascall

Baron von Richthofen
Urped often and hicked often.
His friends knew what do to.
They would sneak up behind him and go Boo.

George Starbuck

Richard Wagner
Was a notorious bargainer:
He got all his singers (both high and deep)
On the cheap.

Edmond Kapp

Archbishop Wareham
Shocked the canons of Sarum
By wearing lace
All over the place.

E. L. Mascall

Waring and Gillow
Liked to share one very small pillow,
A practice which Gillow and Waring
Were inclined to think a little daring.

Martin Knapp

Watteau
Was painting a nymph in a grotto.
He put up a notice 'Défense de toucher'
To warn off Boucher.

J. Griffith Fairfax

Weber
Disliked his neighbour.
He said in advance
'*Don't* come to the dance!'

Eileen Woodland

H. G. Wells
Foretells
Many awful things that came true.
He missed out on The Who.

J. A. Coleman

Miss Mae West
Is one of the best:
I would rather not
Say the best what.

E. W. Fordham

Mrs Whitehouse
Hates the sight of a lighthouse.
To her even a thimble
Is a phallic symbol.

W. F. N. Watson

Mrs Mary Whitehouse
Caught sight of a lighthouse.
It did not escape her detection,
That erection.

Bill Freeman

Oscar Wilde
Was often reviled
For his curious way
Of making the Nineties gay.

Leslie Relsanks

William the Bastard
Frequently got plastered
In a manner unbecoming to the successor
Of Edward the Confessor.

'Lakon'

If anyone could make an op.
Pop.,
Sir Henry Wood
Could.

attrib. Monica Ewer

Lady Mary Wortley Montagu
Refused to use the *accent aigu.*
This whim, which her friends thought curious,
Made the French furious.

Jacques Barzun

W. B. Yeats
Was paid for his poems at very low rates;
It was only thanks to Lady Gregory
That he wasn't reduced to beggary.

John Adlard

William Butler Yeats
Took a poor Third in Greats.
The blame, he told his don,
Lay with Maud Gonne.

Brian Inglis

W. B. Yeats
Was given several crates
And revelled in Guinness, free
On the Lake Isle of Innisfree.

Cecil Hardy

· MAVERICKS AND ·
· SEQUENCES ·

★

COMPOSERS IN CLERIHEW

If Rossini
Was no libertine, he
Was certainly one for the girls
With his liquid eyes and his curls.
(Query:
His relations with *L'Italiana in Algeri*?)

Handel
Thought it an absolute scandal
The way Bach
Cashed in on the *Passions* lark;
It was always a special yen of his
To compose a setting for Genesis.

'Hi ya?'
Said Ravel to de Falla.
'Okay. You well?'
Said de Falla to Ravel:
Neither liked to confess
That he couldn't care less.

It drove Scarlatti
Absolutely batty
To think that what made his
Reputation was *The Good-Humoured Ladies*;
He would far rather have been a
Sort of poor man's Palestrina.

Apparently Johann Strauss
Was an incurable souse.
But can you b-
elieve *The Blue Danube*
Was composed by a guy
Who was perpetually high?

It was a happy illusion of Brahms
That if he'd exerted his charms
On Jenny Lind
She might well have sinned.
Instead he taught Clara Schumann
That to err was human.

Giuseppe Verdi
Admitted that a bird he
Once saw displaying her garter
Was the inspiration for *Traviata*.
It's only a rumour
That he cribbed the idea from Dumas.

Nicolas Bentley

A picture of J. Paul Getty
Walking his dog along a jetty
Was captioned: 'One of these is excessively rich;
The other is a son of a bitch
(No prizes for identifying which is which).'

Charles Maude

THE LITERARY WORLD

*A Collection of Clerihews for Gavin Ewart
on his Sixty-Fifth Birthday*

The influence of Tuscan
Art on Ruskin
Excused what Lawrence
Thought of Florence.

★

Alan Ross
Gathers no moss
As he rolls round the globe
In his bathrobe.

★

In William Trevor's pages
They sing 'Rock of Ages'
By bicycle lamps
Of very few amps.

★

Thou shalt not mock
The verse of Brock,
Nor deprecate
That of Thwaite.

★

Up in Manchester
They don't 'place' *Grantchester*
Until Davie and Sisson
Have given permission,

But they worry a lot,
Especially about what
Schmidt said was greater,
Early Sisson or Later.

★

EDITH SITWELL

Edith Sitwell
Didn't write a bit well
But she looked a right Toff in
An open coffin,

While John Donne allowed
His portrait in a shroud
To remind him before times
Of the true end of all rhymes.

★

Though Jon Silkin will talk
Of the Massacre at York
There's no honour to a prophet
In his own Tophet.

★

Seamus Heaney
Said 'Don't be a meanie,
It's in the Fates,
I'm heir to Yeats.'

★

Among famous names
Few rival Clive James;
Not even Martin Amis
Is quite so famous.

★

Nothing nice
Was said about Rice,
Nor anything clever
About Lloyd-Webber.

★

Said Chris Reid to Craig Raine
'I think it's plain
What you and I write
Is a real look-alike.'

★

Morrison and Sweetman
Are both neat men
Nor will Andrew Motion
Cause any commotion.

★

In Oporto
You can't buy *Quarto*
Or pick up a copy
In downtown Skopje.

★

Tossing the caber
At Faber & Faber
Is as rare as pelota
Played at Bertram Rota.

★

These clerihews
Were written to amuse
That Master of True Art,
Mr Gavin Ewart.

Peter Porter

ARCHITECTURE

Before condemning Nash
For some bit of trash,
You should make perfectly certain
It's not by Decimus Burton.

Sir Charles Bressey
Found London too messy
To make his celebrated report
Short.

The International Style
Had quite a vogue for a while.
But it's hard to turn the tables
On gables.

William Kent
Not without intent
Went to dine with the same men
As Sir Christopher Wren.

The Gothic Revival
Ensured a century's survival
When Barry found a stooge in
Pugin.

Gilbert Scott
Might have been a lovesome thing, God wot,
If he had resisted the wiles
Of the manufacturers of encaustic tiles.

---

3 This name for modernist architecture was
invented in the Thirties by Henry-Russell Hitchcock,
of the Museum of Modern Art in New York.

Mendelssohn and Chermayeff
Cantilevered for dear life
In their endeavours to vie
With Gropius and Fry.

I do not like Pont Street Dutch
Much,
Preferring the more stuccoed behaviour
Of Belgravia.

The great chateaux of old
Leave some people cold.
I, for one, would give Amboise
Une framboise.

The Duke of York's column
Is a trifle too solemn.
I want a teeny
Touch of Bernini.

The Egyptian Style
Has left the Nile
For the banks
Of the Ostrers and Ranks.

These were first published as a sequence in *Clerihews*, the second, enlarged edition of 1946, edited by John Carter. The clerihews were written by: Nicolas Bentley (Chateau d'Amboise), Brooke Crutchley (the Gothic Revival), Lewis Curtis (the Duke of York's column), Hardy Amies (the Egyptian Style), and by John and Ernestine Carter in collaboration (John Nash, Sir Charles Bressey, The International Style, William Kent, Gilbert Scott, Messrs Mendelssohn and Chermayeff, Pont Street Dutch).

MUSICAL HISTORY

Madame von Meck
Said 'Heck –
Next time I'll be wary
Of falling for a Sugarplum Fairy!'

103

Thomas Tallis
Said 'I bear Byrd no malice,
Unless he starts
Writing motets in 40 parts.'

Bach's matrimonial affairs
Involved 2 wives and 20 heirs;
That he kept a spinster in the attic, too,
Isn't true.

Clara Schumann
Was the only woman
Whose charms
Appealed to Brahms.

Claude Debussy
Was always chasing pussy,
But I'd rather not tell
About the pursuits of Ravel.

J. S. Bach
Said 'I don't care about Luke or Mark,
But Matthew and John
Are definitely ON.'

Carlo Gesualdo, Prince of Venosa,
Was a thoroughly modern composer:
Even down to the fact
That he caught his wife and his best friend in the act.

Fritz Spiegl

CENTENARIES

'Instead of *Rainbow*,' said Lawrence,
'I'll call it *Torrents*:
With a barometrical title
Accuracy is vital.'

'If you go a-courtin'
There's one thing that's certain,
You'll need your umbrellas.'
Said gamekeeper Mellors.

Said Lawrence's mother,
'Though darkness is other,
Adding the suffix "-ness"
Gets the syntax in a mess.'

Lawrence's father
Said 'I'd much rather
Miss the hocus-pocus
And join the smoking jokers.'

Said Frieda, 'It's enough to vex
Oedipus Rex:
Sooner or later,
It was me or the mater.'

Said Lawrence's Frieda,
'I'm fond of Lieder,
But of *Tipperary*
I'm a bit wary.'

D. H. Lawrence
Married 'one of the foreigns':
His Ursulas
Thus got worse – alas!

Ursula Brangwen
Wasn't sanguine
That Rupert Birkin
Would go on working.

The bark of Gerald Crich
Was much worse than his bite –
The actor Oliver Reed
Seems to have disagreed.

Said Lawrence, 'Admittedly,
I'm fond of Italy,
Though I may go
To Tierra del Fuego.'

He avoided come-uppance
By living on tuppence,
But now things Lawrentian
Are well worth a mention . . .

. . . And *Lady Chatterley*
Has sold well latterly.
'What the hell!'
Says D.H.L.

Donald Measham

2 Crich *is pronounced* Crite-ch.

FIRST AID FOR EXAMINEES

Jonathan Swift
Wouldn't take a wife as a gift;
He preferred living singly
In spite of Rebecca Dingley.

Thomas Gray,
A gem of purest ray,
Was not at all serene
When forced to blush unseen.

William Cowper
Is no longer regarded as super;
His verses neither cheer
Nor inebriate, I fear.

Edward Gibbon
Wore a pigtail tied with a ribbon;
Almost nobody reads all
Of his great *Decline and Fall*.

Sir Walter Scott
Is a lovesome poet, God wot,
For those who like maidens on islands
In damp inaccessible Highlands.

Jane Austen
Would have felt at home in Boston;
She would go to the beach in Dorset
And never take off her corset.

Charles Lamb
Said 'D-d-d-d-d-d-damn!
I really think this stutter
Makes wittier what I utter.'

Walter Savage Landor
Was fiercely addicted to candor;
In spite of his daily rage
He lived to a cross old age.

George Gordon, Lord Byron,
Had a constitution of i-ron;
His sex life was always strenuous
And his hold on morality tenuous.

Alfred, Lord Tennyson,
Was always invoking a benison
On something of no use at all,
Like a flower in a crannied wall.

Charles Dickens
Said 'When the plot thickens,
I have to explain what it all meant
As I write the next instalment.'

Algernon Charles Swinburne
Felt flaming passions of sin burn;
He needed the help of Watts-Dunton
To keep a respectable front on.

H. Rider Haggard
Was certainly no laggard;
He dreamed up the heroine She
For the cinema rated 'B'.

Pearl S. Buck
Had rather a lot of luck:
Though her prose is not aureate,
She made Nobel Laureate.

Richard Leighton Greene

SELECTED FROM 'HOMAGE TO E. C. BENTLEY'

Though William Cullen Bryant
Like Emerson was self-reliant,
He acknowledged and was proud to mention
His debt to waterfowl and the fringed gentian.

Emerson (Ralph Waldo)
When he was called ('O
Waldo!') by the Oversoul,
Yielded himself to the perfect Whole.

The desire electric, superb, of Walt Whitman's
Self imperturbe was to knit Man's
Osirian fragments – heart, mind, soul, and sex terrific –
Into a seamlessness squarely deific.

A grim conceit of Edgar Lee Masters
Took this form: after Spoon River pastors
Had buried such as turned down an empty cup,
He dug them up.

William Carlos Williams
Runs barefoot through the trilliums,
A sensuous epistemologist who sings
'Wake, robin, say it: no ideas but in things.'

Let the heavens resound
For Ezra Pound
Who wrought with his unfailing ear
110　The splendor of cantos that don't cohere.

A fact of life for Adrienne Rich is
That men are mostly sons-of-bitches.
Many agree, but there are others
Who ask: If so, what are their mothers?

God's spy, John Milton
Squarely placed the primal guilt on
Women's shoulders, who merely smiled away his frown,
Taking it lightly – lying down.

Alexander Pope
Discovered in the couplet heroic scope:
Tea-party rape, Troy toppled, Dullness regnant,
Abelard unmanned, Man studied, and Lord Fanny pregnant.

Samuel (Dictionary) Johnson
Kowtowed to no Hon and to no Hon's son
And through his life's vicissitudinal course
Was now an immovable object, now an irresistible force.

The navigational feats of Francis Drake
Look small by those of William Blake,
Whose acquaintance with infinity
Equalled that of the Trinity.

Upon what meat doth this our Percy Shelley,
Our Ariel, feed his bowels and belly?
On that which nourished Cupid and his Psyche
And, before she was beheaded, Nike.

That large utterance of John Keats,
Despite a schoolboy taste for sweets
(Not least of which was Mrs Brawne's daughter),
Assured a name writ large in holy water.

111

112   **DYLAN THOMAS**

To heal the modern malady, Matthew Arnold
Prescribed Sweetness and Light, and tried to warn old
Philistines and new to accept no substitutes. He failed. The
   medicine
They chose was Hershey's Sweetness and the Light of
   Edison.

Poems of Robert Bridges –
Were they prepared in ovens or fridges?
Both. A hot meringue was made to mask a
Heart of ice cream, as in baked Alaska.

It does not matter, says A. E. Housman.
However lass, lad, lady, mouse, man
Twists or turns, Death springs the trap.
And guess who's there to hear the neck-bone snap.

Wystan Hugh Auden
In his late poems said 'Praise God' in
More ways than one would think
Fitting in an erstwhile Parlor Pink.

Dylan Thomas
Never read about Vasco da Gama's
Adventures, preferring erotic magazines' juicy ads
To the Lusiads.

Clark Emery

113

OMAR KHAYYAM

Omar Khayyam
Thought ethics a sham.
He saw nothing wrong
With wine, women and song.

Of course, Omar K.
Was just made that way –
He couldn't decline
Song, women or wine.

Poor Khayyam! Oh
What did he know
About tennis or swimming? –
Just song, wine and women.

Wendy Cope

PHILOSOPHICAL CLERIHEWS

Aristotle
Took to the bottle
When he found, after all he'd been through,
No End in view.

In the end, Gottlob Frege
Got vaguer und vaguer
Until even ze names of his friendz
No longer made zenz.

When Ludwig Wittgenstein
Had too much wine
Bertie's set
Thought him rather wet.

Ronald de Sousa

SELECTED FROM 'SCURRILOUS CLERIHEWS' IN
'NIGHT THOUGHTS'

The Paradox of Thornton Wilder

Thornton Wilder
Couldn't be milder;
And yet, by gracious,
He's rather erinaceous.

John Dos Passos, Esqre

John Dos Passos
No longer writes for the Masses,
And when he returns to his Virginia estate, he
 is greeted by a chorus of 'Old Massa!'s.
On account of Soviet knavery
He favours restoring slavery.

The Tates

Allen Tate
Is slightly out of date –
As is his devoted mate,
Caroline Gordon Tate.

Metternich's Great Admirer

Clever Peter Viereck'll
Seem a bit more of a miracle
If he'll hold himself in a particle
And refrain from sending us offprints of his every godblessed
 article.

Edmund Wilson

OLIVER TWIST

Oliver Twist
Stands high on the list
Of the characters of Dickens
Of whom the reader readily sickens.

And the lovely Rose
Is another of those
Whose impact is not so much pathetic
As emetic.

And even Nancy,
Though her morals were, to say the least, chancy,
Seems just a little bit too
Dam good to be true.

Robert Baird

NOTES AND QUERIES

John Donne,
Being long since gone,
Cannot confirm whether one
Should pronounce it Donne.

Ditto Thomas Carew:
Would that one knew
If he allowed it to vary,
Or answered only to Carew.

Jonathan Price

EYE-RHYME CLERIHEWS

Sir Edmund Gosse
Was arrested by a posse
Of remarkably nice
Police.

E. W. Fordham

Thucydides
Seldom laughed till he split his sides,
And was thus one of the banes
Of Aristophanes.

R. S. Stanier

Euripides
Was an old sobersides,
He made no ribs ache
With his *Andromache*.

Joyce Johnson

Alfred de Musset
Would eat no apples but russet,
Which Debussy
Regarded as ridiculously fussy.

F. Galway

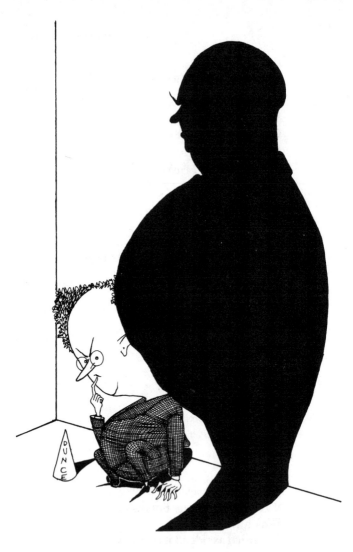

Auberon Waugh
Makes some people laugh,
But fewer, I gather,
Than his father.

F. Galway

NEWSPAPERS AND PERIODICALS

Woman's Own
Now dispenses sexual advice with a certain tone,
And considerably more decorum
Than *Forum*.

Cyril Hughes

The *Pig Breeders' Gazette*,
I bet,
Is full of fascinating talk
About pork.

Cyril Hughes

Screen
Isn't the magazine
For those at variance
With the Althusserians.

Basil Ransome-Davies

The *Sun*
Has a simple idea of fun:
It's
Tits.

Basil Ransome-Davies

The *Sun* is far from being niminy-
Piminy;
More Hammery-
Mammary.

Stanley J. Sharpless

119

The TLS
Never says succinctly No! or Yes!
It elaborates the causes
In relative clauses.

Gavin Ewart

The *Morning Star*
Would far
Rather be read
Than dead.

Stanley J. Sharpless

You only read *Pravda*
Because you havda:
There's not much sport
But a lot of political thort.

Bill Greenwell

When it comes to the crunch
The trouble with *Punch*
Is that that's precisely the quality it's not
Got.

Martin Fagg

HOLIDAY RESORTS

Any Gentleman can be seen tight on
The promenade at Brighton:
But – by Jove,
If it happened at Hove!

J. D. K. Lloyd

Perranporth
Should be moved north.
It would be best
If it went west.

G. McD. Wilson

The *little* theathide platheth
Have never been much in my good gratheth.
But I *love* Bournemouth –
Itth tho enormouth.

L. G. Udall

If Devon
Is really a bit of Heaven
I can't help being disappointed
With some of the Lord's anointed.

Percy Vere

I've always looked askance
At Penzance
And thought
'It's the last resort.'

Stanley J. Sharpless

Southend-on-Sea
Is not for the likes of you and me:
It is full of unspeakable heels
Who eat eels.

Cyril Hughes

'INITIAL' ORGANISATIONS

Only a few know
All the members of UNO.
Burma is one, but who knew?
U Nu?

Gloria Prince

The NAAFI
Is a sort of caafi
Where soldiers are rude
About the food.

Allan M. Laing

Tribes
Of scribes
Are PEN
Men.

H. A. C. Evans

What I like about WHO
Is no one knows what they do.
We still wait to be told
The cure for a cold.

Admiral Sir W. M. James

ANIMALS

Take my advice on
Meeting a *Bison*,
Just give a gruff 'Hallo'
And pretend you're a *Buffalo*.

Lionel S. Harris

To enamel
The camel
Would be silly,
Like gilding the lily.

Richard Pomfret

The stag keeps a straight bat;
He's full of *noblesse oblige* and all that.
You may mention to him *The Times*, Landseer, and Tennyson,
But on no account Bradlaugh, the *New Statesman*, or venison.

G. de Vavasour

The stoat
Should take note
That, while in winter it is ermine,
In the summer it's merely vermin.

W. M. Cundall

Weasels
Never suffer from measles;
They can jump, skip, and hop,
And go pop.

C. J. Kaberry

The Scottish stag
Stands on a crag
To be shot by some Saxon
With a name like Jackson.

The desire to give socks
To the fugitive fox
Distinguishes the English upper classes
From the masses.

D. N. Dalglish

The skunk
Has always stunk:
Even her best friends don't seem to know
About BO.

Allan M. Laing

The warthog
Is a kind of bristly, dark, brown, swart hog.
It's not celebrated in song, saga, dithyramb or ditty –
Because it isn't very pretty.

The ardvark
Is an Afrikaans anteater quite opposed to ard vark.
It would like to be lazy –
But to keep alive it has to eat ants like crazy.

Gavin Ewart

PLACES

The town council of Bacup
Are tolerant of make-up:
Even encouraging the Mayor
To peroxide his hair.

The locals at Beaulieu
Are no good to yours truly;
Most of the people of Hants
Need a kick in the pants.

The porters of Newhaven
Though better shaven
Seem to me to have less pep
Than those of Dieppe.

The Chapter of Lincoln
Used to share *The Pink 'Un*.
On its ceasing publication
They fell back on *The New Statesman and Nation*.

T. P. Walker

Sodom and Gomorrah
Were the objects of virtuous horror
Until they received a boost
From Proust.

Ronald Mason

You can't get Watney's
At Totnes,
But Beer
Is quite near.

Bernard D. Smith

127

At Tooting
There is very little shooting;
The birds, you'll find,
Are not that kind.

'Lamsilon'

In Madagascar
Ask her:
'*Est-ce que vous pouvez*
Under a duvet?'

John Gilmour

CLERIHEWS INSULTING TO ACTORS AND ACTRESSES OF
BEAUTY AND TALENT

I'd rather be fed to the lions
Than watch Jeremy Irons:
Actors with just one expression
Induce depression.

Rufus Stone

Wendy Craig's nose
Definitely *grows*
Between episodes of 'Nanny'.
Uncanny!

V. Ernest Cox

129

Diane Keaton
Is easily beaten
For the range of expressions she can muster
By her namesake, Buster.

Charles Hennessy

I wish Faye Dunaway
Would run away;
She's hard to abide
And about as bonnie as the Clyde.

Mary Hardy-Smith

CLERIHEWS ON THE TITLES OR FIRST
LINES OF FAMOUS POEMS

Abou ben Adhem
Increased his tribe with any passing madam
But was not as randy as
Ozymandias.

Ken Claybourne

'Dover Beach'
Doesn't exactly preach.
It just says: 'I've got this gel;
The rest of you can go to hell.'

Colin Falck

'Lines Composed a Few Miles Above Tintern
    Abbey on Revisiting the Banks of the Wye
    During a Tour, 13 July, 1798'
Illustrate
That a title
Isn't vital.

Bill Greenwell

When I was young and twenty
I had plenty
And even had
A Shropshire lad.

Harrison Everard

131

'Little Gidding',
Although forbidding,
Compares
Favourably with Pam Ayres.

Nicholas Murray

Of Man's first disobedience and the fruit
Nobody thinks – or cares a hoot.
Nor does anyone much believe
In Adam, the Serpent, or Eve.

Gavin Ewart

AUSTRALIANS

Sir Joseph Banks
Filled in a lot of botanical blanks.
From his earliest years he'd been anxious
To discover banksias.

H. V. Jacques

Helpmann (Sir Robert)
Is *not* a hobbit.
A hobbit is a species of fairy,
And its feet are not small and neat but large and hairy.

Tess van Sommers

The loss of Harold Holt
Was a jolt.
No gags.
Just swim between the flags.

John Muir

Dame Nellie Melba
Sang everywhere except Elba.
She is remembered most
For peach puddings and thin toast.

John Muir

3 Harold Holt was the Australian Prime Minister who mysteriously disappeared while bathing off an Australian beach. No trace of him was ever found. Australian beach authorities will take no responsibility for you if you swim outside the marker flags.

The Reverend Frederick Nile
Shuns what is vile;
Even to think about such things he daren't:
How come he's a parent?

Renata Ratzer

Even our famous John Singo
Can't compete with that dingo,
Whose international fame grows ever starrier
Since eating Azaria.

Renata Ratzer

1 Nile is an Australian protector of morals.

2 John Singleton is a noted Australian mediaman (advertising, TV, radio). Azaria was the infant daughter of a couple called Chamberlain, who claimed that she had been carried off by a dingo at Ayer's Rock. They were later charged with murder.

CANADIANS

William Lyon Mackenzie King
Did an unusual thing.
He used a notorious mother fixation
To become the father of his nation.

Margaret Trudeau's
Books win no kudos
As art, but about her physical
Charms all Canadian men are now quizzical.

René Lévesque
Smokes cigarettes avec
Monumental disdain
Again and again.

Janet and Barry Baldwin

L'honorable Marc Lalonde
Ressemble beaucoup à tout le monde,
Sauf qu'il sourit quand il pense
Au prix de l'essence.

Edward Baxter

1 Mackenzie King (Canada's Prime Minister during the Second World War) held office at various times between 1921 and 1948. His personal papers have revealed an interest in spiritualism. In particular, his political decisions were influenced by 'communications' from his dead mother.

2 Margaret Trudeau, separated wife of Prime Minister Pierre Trudeau, wrote two books, *Beyond Reason* and *Consequences*, describing her rebellion against public life. They describe drug experience and love-affairs with American film stars such as Jack Nicholson and Ryan O'Neill.

3 René Lévesque is the leader of the Parti Québécois, advocating the separation of Quebec from Canada. Premier of Quebec since 1976, he is an extremely heavy smoker.

4 Marc Lalonde is the current (1982) Canadian Minister of Energy. During his tenure of office the price of petrol/gasoline has increased dramatically.

135

Acknowledgements

MANY of the clerihews assembled here were submitted as entries in a clerihew competition organized by Godfrey Smith for the *Sunday Times*.

Other competitions have also been ransacked for this collection, organized by *Books and Bookmen*, *Books in Canada*, *New Statesman*, *The Spectator* and *The Sydney Morning Herald*, to mention the main sources. Clerihews from these appear here and my acknowledgements are due to the Editors of these periodicals. I am also indebted to *The Pauline*, the magazine of St Paul's School.

Some clerihews appeared in papers that don't exist any more, and in publications like *The Saturday Book*. My thanks are also due (posthumously as it were) to the Editors of these.

Acknowledgements are due to all the individual clerihewers, or estates where appropriate, who have given permission for work to be published. If there are any authors I have not been able to trace, perhaps they would write in?

Acknowledgements are also due to the following for permission to reprint copyright material:

André Deutsch, on behalf of Mrs Nicolas Bentley, for clerihews by Nicolas Bentley: Cecil B. de Mille, Debenham & Freebody and Amboise from *Clerihews*, edited by John Waynflete [Carter], second edition (see bibliographical note below); Rossini, Handel, Ravel, Scarlatti, Johann Strauss, Brahms and Verdi from *The Saturday Book No 18*, edited by John Hadfield (Hutchinson, London, 1947).

Faber & Faber Ltd and Random House Inc. for Henry Adams, William Blake, Arthur Hugh Clough, Fulke Greville, Luther & Zwingli and Thomas Moore from *Academic Grafitti* by W. H. Auden, copyright © 1960, 1971, 1972 by W. H. Auden.

Farrar, Straus & Giroux Inc. for the Paradox of Thornton Wilder, John Dos Passos, Esqre, the Tates and Metternich's Great Admirer from 'Scurrilous Clerihews' in *Night Thoughts* by Edmund Wilson, copyright © 1953, 1961 by Edmund Wilson.

David R. Godine Publishers Inc. and the author for Baron von Richthofen and Rabindranath Tagore from *Desperate Measures* by George Starbuck (Godine, 1978), copyright © 1978 by George Starbuck.

ACKNOWLEDGEMENTS

Lescher & Lescher Ltd. for Jacobean by Clifton Fadiman, first published in *The New Yorker* (1956).

William Jay Smith for William Penn from *Mr Smith and Other Nonsense* (Seymour Lawrence/Delacorte Press, 1968), copyright © 1968 by William Jay Smith.

George Weidenfeld & Nicolson Ltd for Christopher Logue by Kenneth Tynan.

Bibliographical note – additional sources
The books listed below all contain clerihews of merit (some of them included in this volume) as well as other light verse of a high standard.

Anse on Island Creek by Paul Curry Steele (Mountain State Press, Charleston, 1981)

Clerihews, edited by John Waynflete [Carter] (Rampant Lions Press, Cambridge, 1938; second edition 1946)

The Fifty-two Clerihews of Clara Hughes by Jonathan Williams (Pynon Press, Atlanta, 1983)

Grave Epigrams and Other Verses by John Sparrow (The Cygnet Press, Burford, 1982)

Pi in the High by Eric L. Mascall (The Faith Press, London, 1959)

Pith and Vinegar, edited by William Cole (Simon & Schuster, New York, 1959)

G. E.

Index of Authors